CW00501876

Trace and W
Hindi Alphabets

An Activity Book
(Trace and Write Hindi Vowels and Consonants)

Step by Step Guide Trace Alphabets

Learn Hindi Through English Series

Designed & Compiled

By

Chandra B. Singh

ISBN: 9798636260332

Note: This book has black and white interior. Book with colored interior has also been published on Amazon. If you need colored version, you can buy at Amazon online portal.

If you like this book and was useful for you then please leave a review on Amazon. Thank you

Hindi Vowels

स्वर

Trace and write Hindi Alphabets – An Activity Book

अ- (A)

A as in America

Steps to write letter "अ"

?	3	3	उ-	अ	अ

अनार Anaar
(Pomegranate)

आ-(AA)

A as in Art

आम Aam
(Mango)

Steps to write letter "आ"

२	3	3	अ	अ	आ

Name :...........................   Date: ....

इ-(I)

I as in India

Steps to write letter "इ"

෭	௨	ड	इ	इ

इमली Imali
(Tamarind)

(five rows of dotted tracing practice for the letter इ)

Trace and write Hindi Alphabets – An Activity Book

Name :............................

 ई-(EE) ee as in Feet

Steps to write letter

ᴸ	ᴸ	ऽ	ऽ	इ	ई

ईख Eekh

(Sugarcane)

Trace and write Hindi Alphabets – An Activity Book

Name : ....

Date: ....

उ-(U)

U as in Put

Steps to write letter "उ"

゜	3	उ

उल्लू Ulloo
(Owl)

Name :................................

Date: ....

ऊ-(OO)

oo as in Spoon

Steps to write letter "ऊ"

ʾ	3	उ	ऊ

ऊन Oon
(Wool)

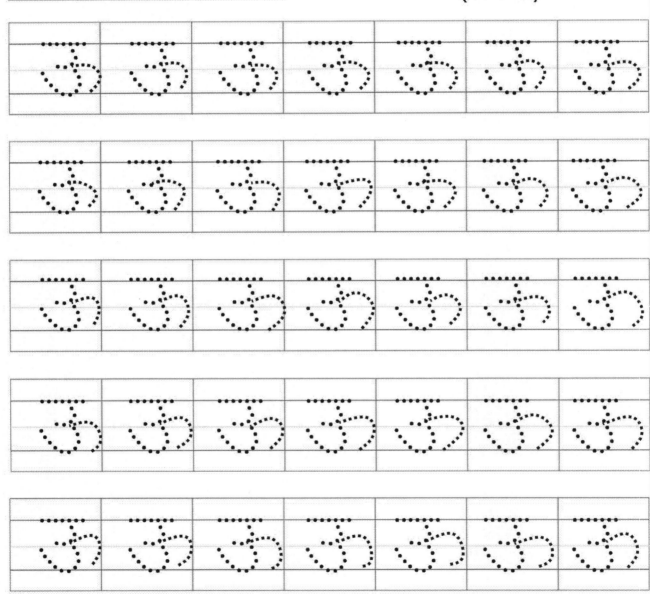

ऋ -(RI)

Ri as in Rib

Steps to write letter "ऋ"

—	T	ञ्र	ऋ	ऋ

ऋषि Rishi
(Sage)

Name : ....

Date: ....

ए-(AE)
AE as in Aerobics

1

एक Aek
(One)

Steps to write letter "ए"

—	ए	ए

Name : ....

Date: ....

 ऐ_(AI)

AI as in Kaif

Steps to write letter "ऐ"

—	ए	ए	ऐ

सैनिक Sainik
(Soldier)

ओ-(O)

O as in Orange

मोर Mor
(Peacock)

Steps to write letter "ओ"

౨	౩	౩	उ	अ	अ	आ	ओ

Name : ....

Date: ....

औ-(AU)

Au as in Aura

Steps to write letter "औ"

౨	3	3	अ	अ	आ	औ

औरत Aurat
(Women)

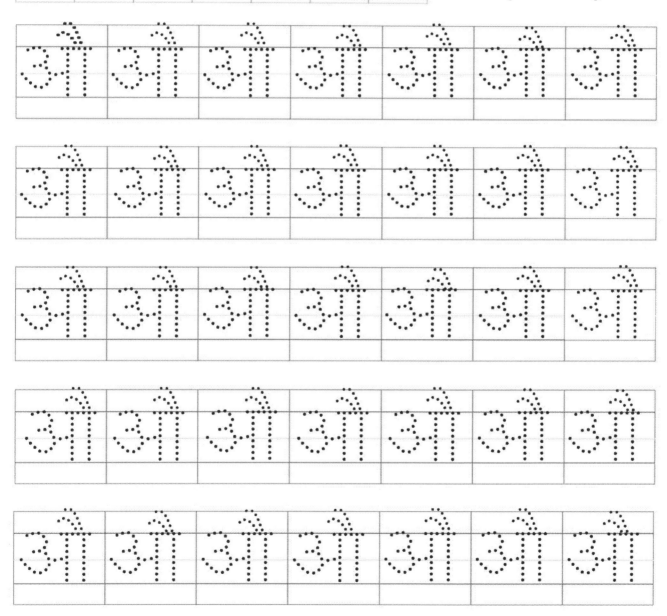

Name :..................................   Date: ....

अं - (UN)

Un as in Hunger

Steps to write letter "अं"

२	3	3ˋ	अ	अ	अं

अंगूर Angoor
(Grapes)

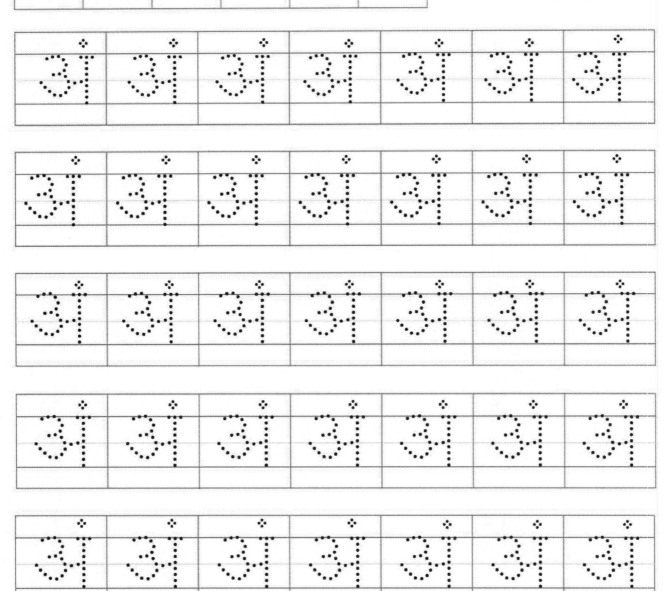

Name : ....   Date: ....

अः -(AH)

Rare use in English

अः

Steps to write letter **"अः"**

ͻ	3	3	अ	अ	अः

पुनः Punah
(Again)

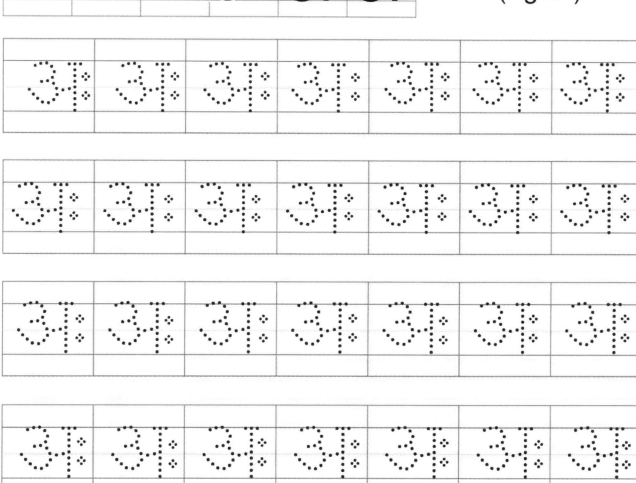

Trace and write Hindi Alphabets – An Activity Book

Vowels स्वर

अ आ इ ई

उ ऊ ऋ ए

ऐ ओ औ अं

अः

Hindi Consonants

व्यंजन

Name :..   Date: ....

क-(Ka)

Ka as in Kadoka

कबूतर Kabūtara
(Pigeon)

Steps to write letter "क"

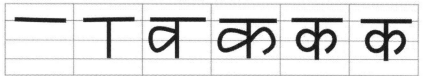

Trace and write Hindi Alphabets – An Activity Book

Name :......................................

Date: ....

ख-(Kha)

Kha as in Khan

खरगोश Kharagōśa
(Rabit)

Steps to write letter "ख"

—	⊐	र	रा	रव	रव

ग-(Ga)

Ga as in Gate

गमला Gamala
(Flower Pot)

Steps to write letter "ग"

—	ऊ	ग	ग	ग

घ-(Gha)

Gha as in Ghost

घड़ी Ghadi
(Watch)

Steps to write letter "घ"

—	ㄱ	प	घ	घ

Name : ....   Date: ....

ङ० - (Anga)

ङ०

Steps to write letter "ङ०"

—	┐	ड	ड	ड०	ङ०

Trace and write Hindi Alphabets – An Activity Book

25

च-(Cha)

Cha as in Chain

Steps to write letter "च"

—	⊐	च	च	च

चम्मच Chammach
(Spoon)

छ-(Chha)

Chha as in Chhap

छाता Chhata
(Umbrella)

Steps to write letter "छ"

| — | ┐ | ट | ट्ट | छ | छ |

Trace and write Hindi Alphabets – An Activity Book

Name : ....

Date: ....

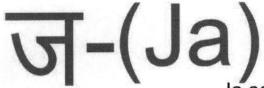

Ja as in Jaguar

Steps to write letter "ज"

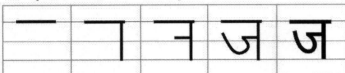

जग Jag
(Jug)

Name : ....

Date: ....

झ-(Jha)

Jha as in Jharna

Steps to write letter "झ"

| — | ┐ | ⊓ | झ | झ | झ |

झंडा Jhanda
(Flag)

Name :...   Date: ....

अ

(ña)

Steps to write letter "अ"

—	⌐	⌐	अ	अ

Trace and write Hindi Alphabets – An Activity Book

Name : ....

ट-(Ta)

Ta as in Talk

टमाटर Tamatar
(Tomato)

Steps to write letter **"ट"**

—	⊤	ट	ट

Trace and write Hindi Alphabets – An Activity Book

Name : ....

Date: ....

ठ-(Tha)

Steps to write letter "ठ"

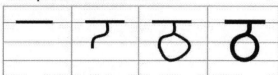

Tha as in Thahro
(a Hindi Word means Stop)

ठठेरा (Thathera)
Tinker

Trace and write Hindi Alphabets – An Activity Book

Name : ....

Date: ....

Da as in Dab

डमरू Damaru
(Pellet Drum)

Steps to write letter "ड"

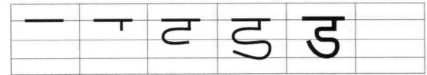

Trace and write Hindi Alphabets – An Activity Book

Name : ....

Date: ....

ढ-(Dha)

Dha as in Dhaka

ढोलक Dholak
(Drum)

Steps to write letter "ढ"

—	⌐	ट	ढ	ढ

Trace and write Hindi Alphabets – An Activity Book

Name :.................................

Date: ....

ण_(na)

Steps to write letter "ण"

—	ण	ण	ण

ण

ṇa (ana)

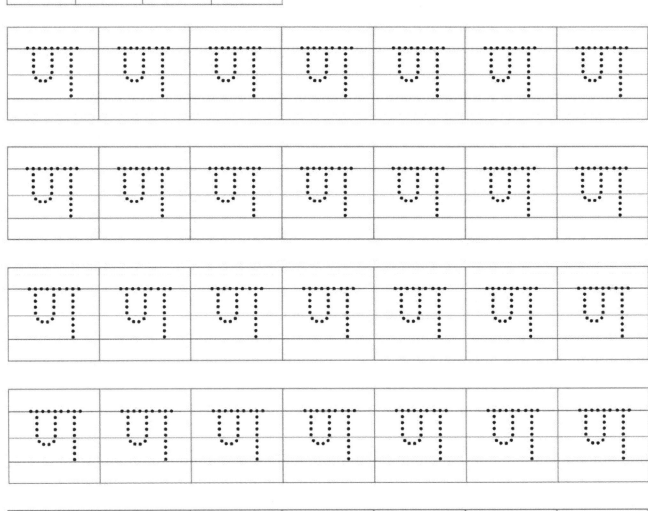

Trace and write Hindi Alphabets – An Activity Book

Name : ....

Date: ....

त-(Ta)

Ta as in Hindi word Talwar

तरबूज Tarbooj
(Watermelon)

Steps to write letter "त"

—	̄ा	त	त

Name : ....

Date: ....

थ-(Tha)

Tha as in Thank

Steps to write letter "थ"

	—	1	ग	घ	थ	थ	

थर्मस Tharmas
(Flask)

Trace and write Hindi Alphabets – An Activity Book

Name : ....

द-(Da)

Da as in Daman

दरवाजा (Darwaja)
Door

Steps to write letter "द"

―	ㅜ	ट	द	द	

Name : ....   Date: ....

ध-(Dha)

Dha as in Dhanbad

धनुष Dhanush
(Bow)

Steps to write letter "ध"

─	ा	ध	ध	ध

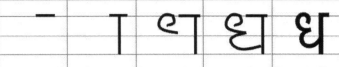

Trace and write Hindi Alphabets – An Activity Book

Name : ....

न-(Na)

Na as in Nasal

Steps to write letter "न"

—	ㄱ	न	न

नल Nal
(Tap)

Trace and write Hindi Alphabets – An Activity Book

प-(Pa)

Pa as in Palm

Steps to write letter "प"

—	ᄀ	प	प

पतंग Patang
(Kite)

Trace and write Hindi Alphabets – An Activity Book

Name : ....

फ-(Fa)

Fa as in Father

Steps to write letter "फ"

—	⊤	प	फ	फ

फल Fal
(Fruits)

Name : ....

Date: ....

ब-(Ba)

Ba as in Banana

Steps to write letter "ब"

—	⊓	ब	ब	ब

बतख Batakh
(Duck)

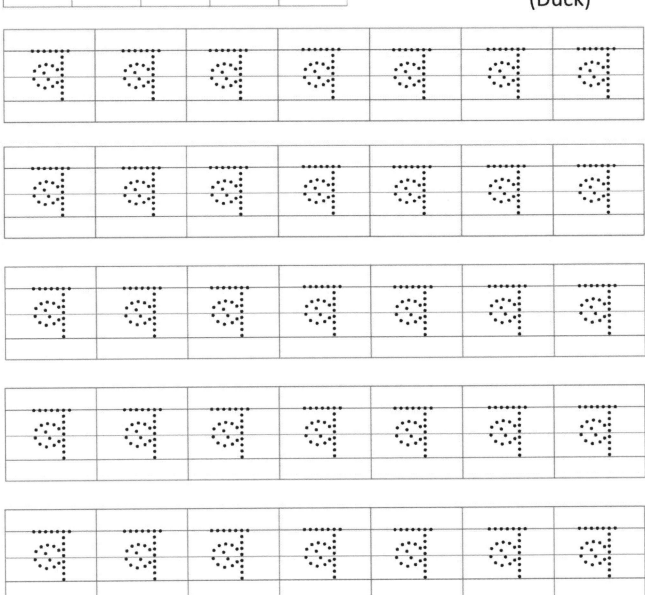

Trace and write Hindi Alphabets – An Activity Book

Name : ....

Date: ....

भ-(Bha)

Bha as in Bharat

भालू Bhaloo
(Bear)

Steps to write letter "भ"

	―	┐	ㄱ	भ	भ

Trace and write Hindi Alphabets – An Activity Book

म-(Ma)

Ma as in March

मछली Machhali
(Fish)

Steps to write letter "म"

—	ㄱ	ㅋ	म

Trace and write Hindi Alphabets – An Activity Book

Name : ....

Date: ....

य-(Ya)
Ya as in Yarn

Steps to write letter "य"

―	ㄱ	ग	य	य

यान Yaan
(Plane)

Trace and write Hindi Alphabets – An Activity Book

Name : ....

Date: ....

र-(Ra)

Ra as in Rag

Steps to write letter "र"

—	ड	र	र

रस्सी Rasse
(Rope)

Name : ....

Date: ....

ल-(La)

La as in Last

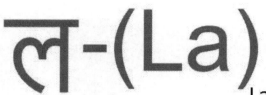

लट्टू Lattoo
(Top)

Steps to write letter "ल"

―	ㄱ	ㄱ	ल	ल

व-(Va)
Va as in Valve

Steps to write letter "व"

—	┐	व	व

वन Van
(Forest)

Trace and write Hindi Alphabets – An Activity Book

Name :.................................

Date: ....

श-(Sha)

Sha as in Shake

शहद (Shahad)
Honey

Steps to write letter "श"

—	ᄀ	ग	श	श

Trace and write Hindi Alphabets – An Activity Book

Name : ....

Date: ....

ष-(sa)

Steps to write letter "ष"

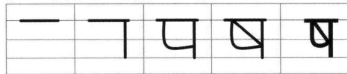

—	٦	प	ष	ष

षट्भुज Shatbhuj
(Hexagon)

Name :...................................

स-(sa)
Sa as in Salon

Steps to write letter "स"

—	ा	रा	सा	स

सब्जी (Sabjee)
Vegetable

Name : ....

Date: ....

ह-(ha)
Ha as in Hall

Steps to write letter "ह"

—	┬	ひ	ह	ह

हाथी Haathi
(Elephant)

Trace and write Hindi Alphabets – An Activity Book

Name :..

Date: ....

क्ष-(Ksha)

Ksha as in Kshatriya

क्षत्रिय (Kshatriya)
Warrior

Steps to write letter "क्ष"

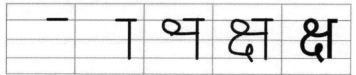

Trace and write Hindi Alphabets – An Activity Book

Name : ....   Date: ....

त्र-(Tra)

Tra as in Trayodash
(Trayodash is Sanskrit Word that means 1

Steps to write letter "त्र"

—	⊤	⊤	त्र	त्र

त्रिशूल (Trishul)
Trident

Name :...   Date: ....

ज्ञ-(Gya)

Gya as in Gyaan

Steps to write letter "ज्ञ"

ज्ञान (Gyaan)
Knowledge

Trace and write Hindi Alphabets – An Activity Book

Consonants व्यंजन

क	ख	ग	घ	ङ
च	छ	ज	झ	ञ
ट	ठ	ड	ढ	ण
त	थ	द	ध	न
प	फ	ब	भ	म
य	र	ल	व	श
ष	स	ह	क्ष	त्र
		ज्ञ		

Trace and write Hindi Alphabets – An Activity Book

Printed in Great Britain
by Amazon

43030000R00033